MW00929370

The CATCHER
El receptor

by Madison Capitano
and Pablo de la Vega

Rourke
Educational Media

A Division of
Carson Dellosa Education

rourkeeducationalmedia.com

BEFORE AND DURING READING ACTIVITIES

Before Reading: *Building Background Knowledge and Vocabulary*

Building background knowledge can help children process new information and build upon what they already know. Before reading a book, it is important to tap into what children already know about the topic. This will help them develop their vocabulary and increase their reading comprehension.

Questions and Activities to Build Background Knowledge:

1. Look at the front cover of the book and read the title. What do you think this book will be about?
2. What do you already know about this topic?
3. Take a book walk and skim the pages. Look at the table of contents, photographs, captions, and bold words. Did these text features give you any information or predictions about what you will read in this book?

Vocabulary: *Vocabulary Is Key to Reading Comprehension*

Use the following directions to prompt a conversation about each word.

- Read the vocabulary words.
- What comes to mind when you see each word?
- What do you think each word means?

Vocabulary Words:		Palabras del vocabulario	
• base runners	• steal	• árbitro	• reflejos
• home plate	• strike zone	• corredores de base	• robar
• reflexes	• umpire	• plato	• zona de strike

During Reading: *Reading for Meaning and Understanding*

To achieve deep comprehension of a book, children are encouraged to use close reading strategies. During reading, it is important to have children stop and make connections. These connections result in deeper analysis and understanding of a book.

 Close Reading a Text

During reading, have children stop and talk about the following:

- Any confusing parts
- Any unknown words
- Text to text, text to self, text to world connections
- The main idea in each chapter or heading

Encourage children to use context clues to determine the meaning of any unknown words. These strategies will help children learn to analyze the text more thoroughly as they read.

When you are finished reading this book, turn to the next-to-last page for **After Reading Questions** and an **Activity**.

Table of Contents

Catchers 4

Skills Behind the Plate 12

Prepare for Impact! 18

So You Want to Be a Catcher? 22

Memory Game 30

Index 31

After Reading Questions 31

Activity 31

About the Authors 32

Índice

Receptores 4

Habilidades detrás del plato 12

¡Prepárate para el impacto! 18

¿Así que quieres ser receptor? 22

Juego de memoria 30

Índice analítico 31

Preguntas posteriores a la lectura 31

Actividad 31

Sobre los autores 32

Catchers

Catchers have a tough job. They squat behind the plate and catch balls from the pitcher. They tag out **base runners**.

base runners (base RUHN-uhrs): players of the team at bat who are attempting to reach a base

— — — — — — — — — —

Receptores

Los receptores tienen un trabajo difícil. Se ponen de cuclillas detrás del plato y atrapan las pelotas que arroja el lanzador. Atrapan a los **corredores de base**.

corredores de base: bateadores que están tratando de llegar a una base

Catcher Bobby Wilson tags out a runner.

El receptor Bobby Wilson atrapa a un corredor.

5

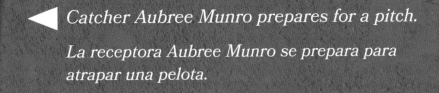

Catcher Aubree Munro prepares for a pitch.

La receptora Aubree Munro se prepara para atrapar una pelota.

Catchers do not wear a regular baseball or softball glove. They use a heavily padded mitt. They also wear protective padding and a catcher's mask.

Los receptores no usan un guante normal de béisbol o sóftbol. Usan un guante muy acolchado. También usan accesorios acolchados y protectores y una careta de receptor.

7

Catchers work hard. They catch pitches and help the pitcher decide what to throw.

- - - - - - - - - - - -

Los receptores trabajan duro. Atrapan lanzamientos y ayudan al lanzador a decidir qué tipo de bola lanzar.

Catcher Tyler Flowers talks with the coach and the pitcher. ▶

El receptor Tyler Flowers habla con el entrenador y el lanzador.

Helping Hand
Sometimes, the pitcher has a hard time. The catcher and the team manager can come to the mound to talk.

— — — — — — — —

Mano amiga
A veces, el lanzador la tiene difícil. El receptor y el entrenador pueden ir al montículo a hablar.

Catchers and pitchers work as a team. They use hand signals to communicate. Catchers use their mitt to give the pitcher a target in the **strike zone**.

strike zone (strike zohn): area over home plate that a pitch must pass to be a strike

— — — — — — — — — — —

Los receptores y los lanzadores trabajan en equipo. Hacen señales con la mano para comunicarse. Los receptores usan su guante para indicar al lanzador un objetivo en la **zona de strike**.

zona de strike (zona de straic): área arriba del plato por la que un lanzamiento debe pasar para hacer un strike

Catcher Wilson Ramos signals the pitcher.

El receptor Wilson Ramos hace señales al lanzador.

11

Skills Behind the Plate

Catchers also throw. Players on the other team can try to **steal** bases. The catcher must throw the ball to stop them.

steal (steel): to steal a base; trying to advance to the next base while the pitcher or catcher is not looking

– – – – – – – – –

Habilidades para el plato

Los receptores también lanzan. Los jugadores del equipo contrario pueden tratar de **robar** una base. El receptor debe arrojar la pelota para detenerlos.

robar: robar una base; intentar el avance a la siguiente base mientras el lanzador o el receptor no están viendo

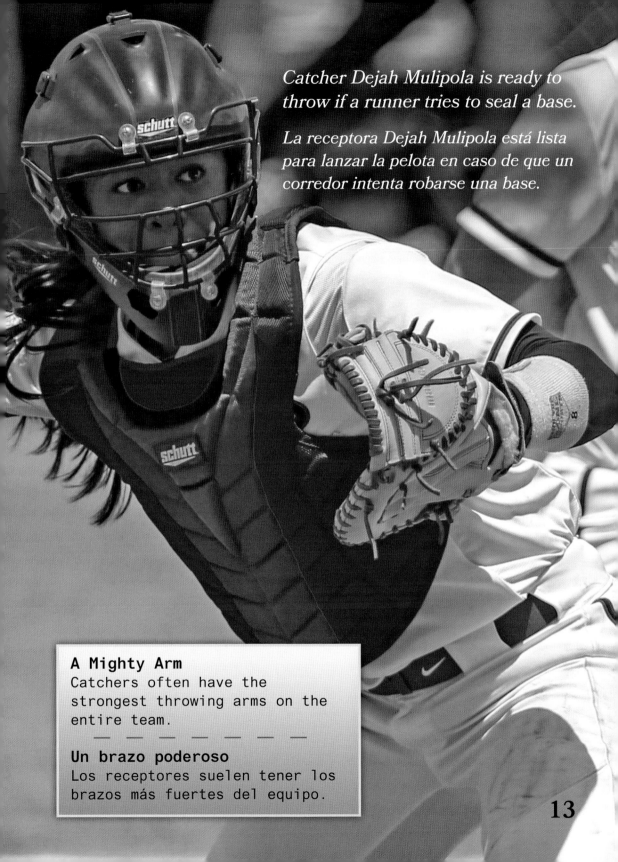

Catcher Dejah Mulipola is ready to throw if a runner tries to seal a base.

La receptora Dejah Mulipola está lista para lanzar la pelota en caso de que un corredor intenta robarse una base.

A Mighty Arm
Catchers often have the strongest throwing arms on the entire team.

— — — — — — —

Un brazo poderoso
Los receptores suelen tener los brazos más fuertes del equipo.

Catchers must focus. It is hard to catch fastballs. They can go 95 miles (152.8 kilometers) per hour. That is very fast!

– – – – – – – – – – – –

Los receptores deben concentrarse. Es difícil atrapar bolas rápidas. Pueden viajar hasta a 95 millas (152.8 kilómetros) por hora. ¡Rapidísimo!

Catcher J.T. Realmuto looks for the ball.

El receptor J. T Realmuto busca la pelota.

Catchers have quick **reflexes**. Sometimes, a batter hits a ball straight up in the air. The catcher jumps up, throws off the mask, and catches the ball before it hits the ground.

reflexes (REE-fleks-iz): actions or movements that happen without effort

– – – – – – – – – – –

Los receptores tienen buenos **reflejos**. A veces, el bateador manda una pelota por los cielos. El receptor brinca, se quita la careta, encuentra la pelota en el aire y la atrapa antes de que caiga al suelo.

reflejos: acciones o movimientos que ocurren sin esfuerzo

17

Prepare for Impact!

Part of the catcher's job is to defend **home plate**. They use their bodies to block pitches. Sometimes, they even block base runners.

home plate (home playt): the base a batter stands next to when hitting; the base a runner must touch to score

- - - - - - - - - - -

¡Prepárate para el impacto!

Parte de su trabajo es defender el **plato**. Usan su cuerpo para bloquear los lanzamientos. A veces también bloquean a los corredores de base.

plato: la base junto a la que se coloca el bateador cuando batea; la base que un corredor de base tiene que tocar para hacer una anotación

18

Catcher Elías Díaz collides with a base runner.
El receptor Elías Díaz choca con un corredor de base.

19

Catchers wear lots of equipment.
This is so they do not get hurt. Masks,
chest protectors, and shin guards keep
catchers safe.

_ _ _ _ _ _ _ _ _ _

Los receptores usan muchos equipamientos.
Esto para no lastimarse. Caretas, protectores
para el pecho y espinilleras mantienen a los
receptores seguros.

All Decked Out
Padding for catchers is also called body
armor. It is similar to the protective
vests that police officers wear.

_ _ _ _ _ _ _

Muy ataviado
Las protecciones para los receptores
son como armaduras. Son similares a los
chalecos antibalas que usan los policías.

Catcher Yadier Molina prepares to throw the ball.

El receptor Yadier Molina se prepara para lanzar la pelota.

21

So You Want to Be a Catcher?

Catchers have the most physically demanding job on the team. They squat, throw, and run. Sometimes, they get hit. But they also have the most exciting seat in the house!

– – – – – – – – – – –

¿Así que quieres ser receptor?

Los receptores tienen el trabajo más físicamente demandante. Se ponen de cuclillas, lanzan y corren. Y suelen recibir golpes. ¡Pero también tienen el mejor asiento!

Catchers play in front of the home plate **umpire**. The umpire peers over the catcher's shoulder. This is the best view of the strike zone for calling balls and strikes.

umpire (UHM-pire): an official who rules on plays in baseball or softball

— — — — — — — — — —

Los receptores juegan delante del **árbitro** del plato. El **árbitro** ve por encima del hombro del receptor para tener la mejor vista de la zona de strike y poder señalar las bolas y los strikes.

árbitro: un oficial que aplica las reglas en el béisbol o el sóftbol

25

It is important for catchers to avoid arguing with the umpire. Catchers can ask questions, but they should be respectful.

— — — — — — — — — —

Es importante que los receptores eviten discutir con el árbitro. Los receptores pueden hacer preguntas, pero de manera respetuosa.

Work Buddies
Catchers and umpires work closely together. Catchers block pitches so the umpire does not get hit. They are friendly!

— — — — — — — — — — —

Compañeros de trabajo
Los receptores y los árbitros deben trabajar muy de cerca. Los receptores bloquean lanzamientos para que estos no golpeen al árbitro. ¡Son amigables entre ellos!

Catcher John Hicks shares a laugh with a home plate umpire.

▶

El receptor John Hicks se ríe con un árbitro del plato.

Do you like playing catch? Do you not mind bumps and bruises? Then grab a mask and some padding. You might make a great catcher!

– – – – – – – – – – – –

¿Te gusta jugar como receptor? ¿No te importa hacerte chichones y raspones? Entonces agarra una careta y protecciones. ¡Podrías convertirte en un gran receptor!

Memory Game / Juego de memoria

Look at the pictures. What do you remember reading on the pages where each image appeared?

— — — — — — — — — —

Mira las imágenes. ¿Qué recuerdas haber leído en las páginas donde aparece cada imagen?

Index

block: 18, 26

chest protectors: 20

mask(s): 7, 17, 20, 28

mitt: 7, 10

pitcher(s): 4, 8, 9, 10, 12

plate: 4, 10, 18, 24, 26

signals: 10

throw: 8, 12, 22

Índice analítico

bloquear, bloquean: 18, 26

careta(s): 7, 17, 20, 28

guante: 7, 10

lanzador(es): 4, 8, 9, 10, 12

lanzamiento: 8, 10, 18, 26

plato: 4, 10, 18, 24, 26

protectores para el pecho: 20

señales: 10

After Reading Questions

1. What are two of the catcher's jobs?
2. What is the strike zone?
3. Name the equipment catchers wear.
4. What does a catcher do if they want to talk to their pitcher?
5. Why is catching hard?

Preguntas posteriores a la lectura

1. Menciona dos funciones del receptor.
2. ¿Qué es la zona de strike?
3. Nombra el equipamiento que usa el receptor.
4. ¿Qué hace un receptor si quiere hablar con el lanzador?
5. ¿Por qué es difícil el trabajo del receptor?

Activity

Imagine you are a catcher. Oh, no–the other team decoded your hand signals! Create three new hand signals to use for communicating with your pitcher.

Actividad

Imagina que eres un receptor. Oh, no: ¡el otro equipo decodificó tus señales manuales! Crea tres señales nuevas para comunicarte con tu lanzador.

About the Authors

Madison Capitano is a writer in Columbus, Ohio. She loves to garden, to travel, and to cook new things. Madison used to read books to her little brother and sister all the time. Now she loves to write books for other kids to enjoy.

Pablo de la Vega wasn't big on sports when he was a kid, but, oh, he loved reading books. Now he watches soccer from time to time when his friends invite him to and loves taking very long walks in cities and in nature. He sometimes translates books for children or finds who can translate them around the world.

www.rourkeeducationalmedia.com

PHOTO CREDITS: Cover: ©; pages 4-5: ©Frank Jansky/Icon Sportswire; pages 6-7: ©Naoki Nishimura/AFLO/Newscom; pages 8-9: ©David J. Griffin/Icon Sportswire ; pages 10-11,16-17: ©Rich von Biberstein/Icon Sportswire ; pages 12-13: ©Jacob Snow/Icon Sportswire ; pages 14-15: ©DennisKu/Shutterstock; pages 18-19: ©Rick Ulreich/Icon Sportswire ; pages 20-21: Arturo Holmes/Shutterstock; pages 22-23: ©Mark Goldman/ICOMSMI; pages 24-25: ©Stephen Hopson/Icon Sportswire; pages 26-27: ©Frank Jansky/Icon Sportswire ; pages 28-29: ©Cynthia Farmer

Edited by: Kim Thompson
Cover design by: Kathy Walsh
Interior design by: Rhea Magaro-Wallace
Translation to Spanish: Pablo de la Vega
Spanish-language edition: Base Tres

Library of Congress PCN Data

The Catcher (El receptor) / Madison Capitano and Pablo de la Vega
(Playmakers in Sports (Jugadores clave en los deportes))
ISBN 978-1-73162-892-3 (hard cover)
ISBN 978-1-73162-891-6 (soft cover)
ISBN 978-1-73162-893-0 (e-Book)
ISBN 978-1-73163-355-2 (e-Pub)
of Congress Control Number: 2019945494

ucational Media
United States of America,
Minnesota